WHAT THE LAND MEANS TO AMERICANS

Alaska and Other Wilderness Areas 1865-1890

TITLE LIST

WHAT THE LAND MEANS TO AMERICANS:
Alaska and Other Wilderness Areas 1865-1890

BY

SHEILA NELSON

MASON CREST PUBLISHERS
PHILADELPHIA

Mason Crest Publishers Inc.
370 Reed Road
Broomall, Pennsylvania 19008
(866) MCP-BOOK (toll free)

First printing
1 2 3 4 5 6 7 8 9 10

Library of Congress Cataloging-in-Publication Data

Nelson, Sheila.
  What the land means to Americans : Alaska and other wilderness areas (1865–1890) / by Sheila Nelson.
      p. cm. — (How America became America)
  Includes index.
  ISBN 1-59084-909-4 ISBN 1-59084-900-0 (series)
  1. Alaska—Annexation to the United States. 2. Alaska—History—1867–1959. 3. Wilderness areas—
Alaska—History—19th century. 4. Landscape assessment—United States—History—19th century. I. Title.
II. Series.
  F907.N45 2005
  979.8'03—dc22
                          2004014361

Design by Dianne Hodack.
Produced by Harding House Publishing Service, Inc.
Cover design by Dianne Hodack.
Printed in the Hashemite Kingdom of Jordan.

CONTENTS

INTRODUCTION

by Dr. Jack Rakove

Today's America is not the same geographical shape as the first American colonies—and the concept of America has evolved as well over the years.

When the thirteen original states declared their independence from Great Britain, most Americans still lived within one or two hours modern driving time from the Atlantic coast. In other words, the Continental Congress that approved the Declaration of Independence on July 4, 1776, was continental in name only. Yet American leaders like George Washington, Benjamin Franklin, and Thomas Jefferson also believed that the new nation did have a continental destiny. They expected it to stretch at least as far west as the Mississippi River, and they imagined that it could extend even further. The framers of the Federal Constitution of 1787 provided that western territories would join the Union on equal terms with the original states. In 1803, President Jefferson brought that continental vision closer to reality by purchasing the vast Louisiana Territory from France. In the 1840s, negotiations with Britain and a war with Mexico brought the United States to the Pacific Ocean.

This expansion created great opportunities, but it also brought serious costs. As Americans surged westward, they created a new economy of family farms and large plantations. But between the Ohio River and the Gulf of Mexico, expansion also brought the continued growth of plantation slavery for millions of African Americans. Political struggle over the extension of slavery west of the Mississippi was one of the major causes of the Civil War that killed hundreds of thousands of Americans in the 1860s but ended with the destruction of slavery. Creating opportunities for American farmers also meant displacing Native Americans from the lands their ancestors had occupied for centuries. The opening of the west encouraged massive immigration not only from Europe but also from Asia, as Chinese workers came to labor in the California Gold Rush and the building of the railroads.

By the end of the nineteenth century, Americans knew that their great age of territorial expansion was over. But immigration and the growth of modern industrial cities continued to change the American landscape. Now Americans moved back and forth across the continent in search of economic opportunities. African Americans left the South in massive numbers and settled in dense concentrations in the cities of the North. The United States remained a magnet for immigration, but new immigrants came increasingly from Mexico, Central America, and Asia.

Ever since the seventeenth century, expansion and migration across this vast landscape have shaped American history. These books are designed to explain how this process has worked. They tell the story of how modern America became the nation it is today.

One
AMERICANS' VIEW OF LAND

After the creation of the world, there were no people or animals. The first man hung curled up inside a peapod for four days. On the fifth day, he stretched out his legs and pushed his feet through the end of the peapod. He fell out onto the ground and stood up. He looked at his arms and legs and moved them around. He felt his neck.

After a while, he started to feel strange. He bent down and drank some water from a small pool. The water ran down his throat and he felt better.

When Man stood up, he saw a dark thing coming toward him. The dark thing stopped in front of him and looked at him. This was Raven. Raven pushed his beak up onto his forehead like a mask and became a man.

"Where did you come from?" Raven asked. "I've never seen anything like you." He was surprised to see how much the man looked like himself.

"I came from that peapod," Man said, pointing at the vine with the broken pod still hanging on it.

"I made that vine!" Raven exclaimed, "but I didn't know anything like you would grow from it. Wait here," he told Man. He pulled his beak back down and became a bird again. Then he flew away, and Man waited for him to return.

Four days later, Raven came back. He pushed his beak up and handed Man four berries. "I

Excesses are extreme indulgences.

Native totem pole

made these for you," Raven said. "I want them to grow everywhere on the earth."

When Man had eaten the berries, Raven took him to a small creek. Man watched as Raven found some clay and formed a pair of tiny mountain sheep.

"Close your eyes," Raven said. When Man had closed his eyes, Raven pulled his beak down and became a bird. He waved his wings four times over the clay figures and they came to life as fully grown mountain sheep.

"Now look," Raven said to Man, pushing his beak up.

Man was delighted with the sheep. Raven made more animals. He made birds and fish. He made insects. So Man would not be lonely, Raven created a beautiful woman for him out of clay. Man loved Woman. He was happy about the creatures that Raven made. More men were growing on the peapod vine. The world was filling up.

Raven watched Man and the other people. He saw how they took pleasure in all the things he made. He started to worry they would eat or destroy everything he had created. Raven decided to create something Man would be afraid of. He took some clay and shaped a bear, flapping his wings over it to make it come alive. Bear stood up on his hind legs and shook himself, roaring fiercely.

"Look," Raven said to Man, "I made this bear. He is very fierce and if you disturb him he will tear you to pieces."

Native peoples across the Arctic regions all tell their own versions of the stories about Raven. Raven is a trickster god, but he is also

A Native artist's interpretation of the connection between bird and orca, spirt and form

creator of the world, bringer of daylight, and teacher of humanity. The stories teach a respect for nature. In the creation story, Raven sees the danger in the natural appetites of Man and cre- ates Bear as a way to counteract Man's ***excesses***.

The Alaska Natives who lived in Alaska before white men came had great respect for the land on which they lived and the nature around them. They understood that the world included things like Bear that were stronger than them and could destroy them. The Native Americans did not think of themselves as owning the land. They lived on the land and used its resources, interacting with nature as a part of nature.

The character of Raven in the stories of the Alaska Natives is both a bird and a man, able to transform from one to the other by moving

his beak up and down. Raven plays tricks on people, but he also teaches them about life and about their place in the world. Raven is a sym-

The Athapascan Indians lived in Alaska before Europeans' arrival

bol of the connection between human beings and nature.

The European settlers did not see the land in the same way as the Native Americans did. More people lived in Europe, and there was less land to go around. Many of the explorers and settlers did not own land in Europe because it was too expensive. When they arrived in North America and realized millions of uninhabited miles stretched before them, they immediately began staking their claims on the new land.

Alaska's untamed wilderness

Eskimo oomiak

The incoming Europeans saw North America as an undiscovered wilderness, a ***frontier*** to be conquered. Nature was harsh—both weather and wild animals could kill the newcomers—but if you survived you could grow huge crops of tobacco or cotton; timber, furs, and gold could make you rich as well. To the Native Americans, this was a completely foreign way of looking at things. Indians saw themselves as a part of nature instead of in conflict with it. They did not view the land as something to be conquered but as something with which to live in harmony.

Most of the Indians already living in the New World did not have permanent settlements. Many were nomadic, hunting and following their game from place to place. The white settlers thought the local tribes did not care about owning the land. More and more Europeans arrived on the shores of North America, moving inland, building roads and towns, and pushing the Indians westward ahead of them onto smaller and smaller ***reservations***. The Native

*A **frontier** is an uncivilized area of land.*

Reservations *are public lands put aside for use by Native Americans.*

15

tribes had little chance of success against the advanced weapons and technologies of the settlers.

For the most part, the settlers thought of North America as uninhabited. They disregarded the existence of the Native Americans, viewing them more as part of the wilderness to be conquered than as people with rights to their own land.

The Founding Fathers of the United States set out to create a great country that was unique in its freedoms and prosperity. They looked at their new country as an experiment, a place where they could build a *democracy* fulfilling all the ideals they felt were lacking back in Europe. One of the most important of these

ideals was individual freedom: a person should have the right to "life, liberty, and the pursuit of happiness."

The New World was huge and rich in resources. Settlers were eager to claim the rights their government told them they had. They wanted to own their own land and become wealthy. Americans came to believe they had a God-given right to spread across the continent and harvest its resources. This idea became known as "Manifest Destiny," after a journalist in 1845 wrote that it

A **democracy** is a form of government in which the will of the majority rules.

17

Providence is another word for God.

Federated means united in an alliance.

was, "the nation's manifest destiny to overspread and to possess the whole of the continent which *Providence* has given us for the development of the great experiment of liberty and *federated* self-government entrusted to us."

In 1867, William Henry Seward, the secretary of state, purchased the huge territory of Alaska from the Russians for 7.2 million dollars. The American people were disgusted. What did they need with over 550,000 square miles of frozen wilderness? Everyone thought Alaska was useless and a waste of money. The American people were *practical* and *materialistic*; if they could not see an immediate material value in a thing, they considered it worthless. Newspapers dubbed the territory Walrussia, Icebergia,

Seward's Icebox, and President Johnson's polar bear garden. The most popular name was Seward's Folly. People thought Seward must have been crazy to spend so much money on such a huge, distant, cold place that—they thought—would be of no use to anyone.

When Seward bought Alaska in 1867, the purchase price worked out to be just two cents per acre!

In spite of the criticism, Seward remained confident that the purchase of Alaska was a good thing for the United States. He believed that the area would "first as a territory, and ultimately as a state or many states, prove . . . worthy as an addition to the United States."

*Someone who is **practical** focuses on the actual use of something.*

*A **materialistic** person believes that worth is connected to the things that one has.*

Peter the Great

Two
ALASKA'S LAND AND HISTORY

Cool breezes gently tugged at the sail of the St. Gabriel, brightly colored against the overcast sky. Vitus Bering stood at the rail and watched as a low dark smudge of land grew larger on the eastern horizon. The Russian expedition had been at sea on the northern Pacific waters east of Siberia for nearly a month, and it was now late August 1728. "I name that land St. Lawrence Island," Bering said, "for my patron saint St. Lawrentius."

Three and a half years earlier, in 1725, Czar Peter the Great had *commissioned* Bering, a Danish sailor serving in the Russian navy, to organize an expedition and discover whether or not Asia and North America were connected by land. Bering was to travel to the northeasternmost part of Russia—Siberia—and from there sail east and north to chart the coastline and learn if Russia bordered North America.

Czar Peter may have already known the truth—the two land masses were not connected. In 1648, a Siberian named Semenn Ivanovich Dezhnev had explored the area and reported that a narrow *strait* separated Russia and North America. Dezhnev's voyage had been over seventy-five years earlier, though, and the records of his exploration had been put away and forgotten about by most

Commissioned means hired to perform a service.

A strait is a narrow passageway connecting two large bodies of water.

One of Bering's charts

people. Even if Peter knew of Dezhnev's discoveries, he could not be completely sure they were accurate. Besides, European exploration and *colonization* in North America was spreading west, and Peter wanted to know if anyone had reached his eastern borders.

Bering took over three years to assemble his party, gather supplies, journey the 5,000 miles across Russia from St. Petersburg to Siberia, and build two ships for the exploration. When he did

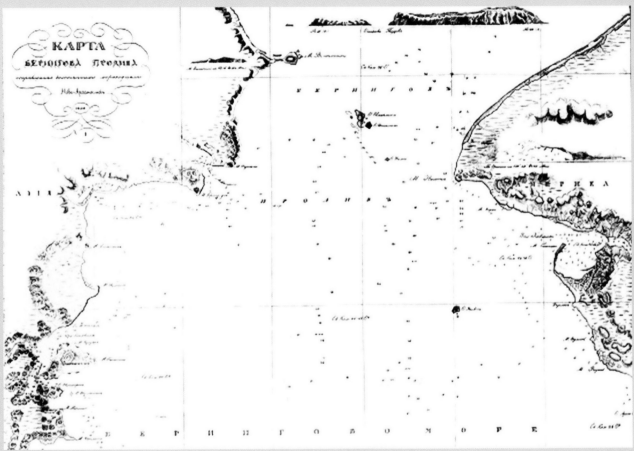

Map of Bering Straits

set out, he was cautious. He knew too much about the harshness of winter and how ships could get trapped in the ice of a frozen sea. He tried to keep the coast of Russia within sight so he could make it to land if weather got bad.

Colonization *means the establishment of a settlement.*

23

St. Lawrence Island was the first non-Russian land Bering and his party spotted. Only thirty-eight miles of sea separated it from Russia's Siberian coast. The explorers did not stop at the island. Even though it was still summer, Bering was nervous about the weather, and he wanted to complete his mission before winter struck.

Bering never saw the mainland of Alaska on this voyage, even though he came within twenty-five miles of it. Fog shrouded the rocky coast, hiding it from view. The group sailed north through what is now the Bering Strait, until the Russian coastline began to turn west. At that point, Bering decided they had accomplished what they had set out to do: They had determined that Russia was not connected to North America. He turned his ships and headed south. On the way back through the strait, Bering caught sight of another island; this one he named St. Diomede.

The next spring, Bering set out to explore the

24

area further, but storms turned him back. After charting part of Russia's Kamchatka Peninsula, he returned to St. Petersburg.

Over a decade later, in 1741, Bering found himself back in Siberia, setting out on another voyage north. This time, his assignment was to map the northern Russian coastline. Seventy-seven men sailed on Bering's ship, the St. Peter, and another seventy-six sailed on the St. Paul, commanded by Alexei Chirikov, Bering's second-in-command. With Bering was Georg Wilhelm Steller, a German scientist who had studied *botany* and medicine.

Bering's third voyage was not as successful as his first. Early in the voyage, a storm drove the two ships, the St. Peter and the St.

Botany *is a branch of biology that studies plant life.*

Reid Glacier

25

A ship battered by a storm

Paul, apart, and Bering could not find them. Many of the crew, including Bering himself, were sick with **scurvy**, making them weak and tired. Adding to Bering's problems was a rivalry between his officers and Steller, the scientist. The sailors disliked Steller, who had a lot of education but very little sea experience. Steller tried to give the men fresh plants to eat to treat the scurvy, but they refused to listen to him.

Late in July 1741, Bering's ship put ashore at a small island off of Alaska's southern coast to get fresh water. Bering named the island St. Elias (today it is known as Kayak Island). They had spent only several hours at the island when Bering announced that they were turning south and returning to Russia.

After six weeks, the expedition had made it only as far as the Shumagin Islands at the end of the Alaska Peninsula. Here, the sailors attempted to get fresh water from a stream, but instead filled their barrels too close to the ocean and ended up with water more salt than fresh. Over the next two months, the *St. Peter* was driven aimlessly across the northern seas, battered by storms The men were too sick with scurvy to even attempt to steer it toward home.

On November 17, the men were finally able to anchor off the shore of one of the Komandorski Islands, near the Kamchatka Peninsula. Less than a month later, a storm threw their ship up onto the beach, destroying it and the rest of their provisions. The group spent the winter on the island, digging holes in the beach and constructing makeshift huts over them for shelter. During the winter, thirty-one men, including Vitus Bering, died of scurvy. In the spring, the survivors built a crude boat from the timbers of

Scurvy is a disease caused by a lack of vitamin C.

Polychrome Pass

Explorers' ships

their ship and made their way slowly to the mainland of Russia. Today, the island where Bering died is named Bering Island in his honor.

Bering's name has become internationally famous since that time. Although many people do not know anything about the explorer himself, they recognize his name from maps: the Bering Strait and the Bering Sea, off the west coast of Alaska, were both named for him.

Despite Bering's connections with the first explorations of Alaska, he never once set foot on the Alaskan mainland. His explo-

ration dealt mainly with the seas and the islands between Russia and Alaska. While Bering investigated the coast, however, Georg Steller took every opportunity to catalogue nature. He discovered and named Steller's jay, the Northern fur seal, the sea otter, Steller's (or Northern) sea lion, Steller's sea cow, Steller's eider, and the spectacled cormorant, among others.

Steller, even more than Bering, would have been delighted to have had the chance to visit Alaska's mainland, where he could have observed still more wildlife. But the Bering expedition saw little of Alaska except for its rocky coast and a few small islands. They never had the opportunity to experience Alaska's variety.

Alaska is huge—almost 600,000 square miles (1,554,000 square kilometers)—and stretches its finger of Aleutian islands over a thousand miles out into the Pacific. Its terrain varies from towering snowcapped mountains—Mount McKinley is the highest point in North America at 20,320 feet (nearly 6,194 meters)—to vast plains of arctic *tundra* to *temperate old-growth rainforests.* Broad rivers flow through its heart; the Yukon is one of the longest rivers in North America. Glacier Bay National Park on Alaska's southeastern arm has jagged *fjords* and towering icy glaciers.

Eskimo of Prince William's Sound, 1728

Alaska's first inhabitants arrived between 30,000 and 15,000 years ago, crossing into North America from Asia on a land bridge exposed by low sea levels during the Ice Age. All the Native American tribes arrived in North America this way, traveling and spreading out slowly south and east. Those remaining in Alaska include the Inupiat and Yup'ik Eskimos, the Aleut, the Athabascans, the Tlingit, and the Tsimshian.

The Inupiat mainly lived along the northwestern coast, near the Bering Strait and north to the Arctic Ocean. They lived in large communities, building houses of sod on wood or whalebone frames, with underground entrances to keep out the cold. They lived on whales, walruses, seals, and caribou.

The Yup'ik lived all along the southern half of Alaska's coasts, from St. Lawrence Island just south of the Bering Strait to Prince William Sound. The more northern Yup'ik depended on seals and whales for food, and those in the south more often caught salmon.

The Aleuts lived on the Aleutian Islands, surviving mainly on sea lions, but also hunting whales and sea otters, and fishing for halibut and cod. They tended to live in small villages, spending time in seasonal fishing camps as well.

Aerial view of Alaska

Tundra is a treeless plain of black mucky soil with a permanently frozen subsoil.

Temperate means to have a moderate climate, not too hot and not too cold.

Old-growth rainforests are ones that are in their natural state; they have not been damaged by human activities such as logging.

Fjords are narrow inlets of the sea between cliffs or steep slopes.

"Alaska" comes from the Aleut word Aleska, meaning "The Great Land."

31

Dog sled

One of Alaska's whales

The Athabascans lived in Alaska's interior, hunting caribou and fishing for salmon. They spent most of their time near the rivers, although they were ***nomadic*** and often followed the ***migration*** of the caribou herds. Their culture was similar to many woodland Native American tribes. They hunted with bows, wore buckskin clothes with fringes and beads, and used birchbark to make canoes and bowls.

The Tlingit lived along the southeastern coast, and the Tsimshian just to the south of them. The tribes built their homes from cedar planks, fished for cod, halibut, herring, and salmon, and hunted seals, deer, moose, and mountain goats.

The cultures of Alaska's Native peoples differed from group to group, but they also had similarities. The most important similarity was that they all survived by living on what nature offered them. The land was everything to them; it gave them the food they needed to live, but kept them balanced between survival and destruction. They lived from the land, although nature was harsh and life was never easy.

Vitus Bering's explorations of Alaska's coastlines signaled coming changes to the Alaska Natives. The second ship in Bering's ill-fated 1741 voyage, the St. Paul, commanded by Aleksei Chirikov, managed to return to the Kamchatka Peninsula that same year. They car-

Athabascan Indians

Caribou

ried with them a load of sea otter pelts and other furs. In western Russia, people's interest in this new land began to be stirred. People could get wealthy from furs like these. Men trickled east to earn their fortunes, moving from island to island along the Aleutians.

As the Russians moved toward Alaska from the west, the Spanish began to move up from the south. Ever since Britain had defeated the Spanish Armada in 1588, Spain's power in the Atlantic had dwindled. On the Pacific coast, however, Spain owned the territory of California, and the Spanish worried when they heard rumors of Britain moving west. They worried even more when they discovered that the Russians were strengthening their position in the north, spreading their colonies southward. To counteract both of these rivals, Spain decided to send their own expedition north.

In 1774 and 1775, Spain sent out preliminary expeditions north

Nomadic *means roaming from place to place, without a fixed pattern of movement.*

Migration *is the passage from one place to another, often on a seasonal basis.*

Legitimize means the process of making legal.

Eighteenth-century Spanish settlement in California

to the Alaska coast. Then, in 1788, Estevan Martinez traveled to Kodiak Island and Unalaska Island in the Aleutians. While there he heard the Russians intended to establish a base on Vancouver Island to the south. Hurrying to lay claim to the island ahead of the Russians, Spain discovered the English had already claimed it. Tensions grew, until at last both sides signed the Nootka Sound Convention in 1790, giving them both the right to use the area, with neither allowed to build a permanent settlement there. The Nootka Sound Convention also included an agreement stating nations now had to build a settlement on the land they claimed in order to *legitimize* that claim.

In 1789, a Spanish expedition led by Alejandro Malaspina sailed north to the area near Mount St. Elias, on Alaska's southeastern coast. When the party discovered Yakutat Bay, they hoped they had found a route north to the Arctic Ocean, but they soon realized this was not the case when they reached a glacier blocking the way further inland. The Spanish group had a number of scientists with them, and they spent some time mapping the area, studying the local wildlife, and observing the Tlingit culture.

Malaspina's expedition was the last major voyage to Alaska funded by the Spanish government. When Malaspina returned to Spain, he angered the king by criticizing his handling of the Spanish colonies. Malaspina was thrown in prison and the records of his exploration were lost for nearly a hundred years.

At nearly the same time as the Spanish, the English began to explore up the coast from the south. At first, they were mostly interested in finding the Northwest Passage, a water route from the Atlantic to the Pacific. In 1776, the British Admiralty sent Captain

Alejandro Malaspina

*A **plateau** is land area with a level surface raised sharply above land on at least one side of it.*

*An **archipelago** is an area of water with a group of islands.*

Cook's voyage to Alaska

James Cook to sail up the northwest coast of North America to look for a western outlet of the passage. In 1778, Cook spent a number of months mapping the Alaska coastline, sailing as far north as Icy Cape on the northwestern coast.

When Cook was killed while wintering in Hawaii, other English captains took over the exploration of Alaska. On the way home to England, one of these men, Captain James King, stopped in Canton, China, for supplies. While he was there, he discovered that the Chinese merchants would pay generously for the sea otter pelts he was carrying. When he returned to England, he reported their interest in northern furs, and news spread that good money could be made in the Alaskan fur trade.

England contributed to the mapping and exploration of Alaska, and some individual trappers settled there, but no English colonies were established on Alaskan soil. England's attention and resources were needed elsewhere, first on the eastern side of North America to deal with the revolution of their American colonies, and then in the drawn-out wars with France.

The French had very little to do with the exploration of Alaska. One of the few French expeditions that traveled north was that of Jean-François de Galaup de la Perouse. La Perouse admired Captain Cook and wanted to follow up on his voyages. In 1782, La Perouse reached the southern part of Alaska, near Mount St. Elias. At first, he was not impressed by what he saw. He wrote that Alaska was a "sterile treeless land . . . a black *plateau*, as though burnt out by some fire, devoid of any greenery, a striking contrast with the whiteness of the snow we could make out through the clouds."

As La Perouse sailed south along the coast, however, his opinion of the land changed. He passed Cape Fairweather and discovered Lituya Bay, a wide passage running east. La Perouse hoped this would be the Northwest Passage, but he soon discovered it was not. Nevertheless, Lituya Bay was beautiful—La Perouse called it "perhaps the most extraordinary place in the world"—and he hoped France could build a base there. He wrote:

> I never saw a breath of air ruffle the surface of this water; it is never troubled but by the fall of immense blocks of ice, which continually detach themselves from fine glaciers, and which in falling make a noise that resounds far through the mountains. The air is so calm that the voice may be heard half a league [two to three miles or nearly three to four kilometers] away.

La Perouse and his men made camp on an island in the middle of the bay and were greeted by a group of friendly Tlingit. The Indians told the Frenchmen that the entrance to the bay could be very dangerous; not long ago they had lost seven large canoes. Soon, the French realized the truth of the Tlingit's words. Two small boats and twenty-one men were lost as they tried to measure the depth of the water at the bay's entrance.

The French left Lituya Bay and continued south, charting some of the islands in the Alexander *Archipelago*, before sailing to

The Russian Orthodox Church

The Russian Orthodox Church left Russia's most lasting impression on Alaska. In the 1800s, the center of that church was Father Ivan Veniaminov, a priest who had been born and raised in Siberia. Father Veniaminov requested an assignment to the Aleutian Islands in 1824. During the time he spent there, he won the respect of the Aleuts. He learned the Aleut language, wrote textbooks and a dictionary in the language, and conducted church services in Aleut. Unlike the early Russians in Alaska, he respected the native culture.

In 1834, the church sent Father Veniaminov to Sitka, where he impressed the Tlingit as much as he had the Aleuts. When he arrived, he offered to immunize the Indians against smallpox. This went a long way toward getting them to trust him.

In 1839, the church made him a bishop—Bishop Innocent. In his new position, he sent out missionary priests who had been trained at the seminary he had built in Sitka. The priests traveled across Alaska by kayak, dogsled, and on foot, building churches and spreading the gospel.

Even after Alaska had been sold to the United States and Russia had officially withdrawn, Russia's presence lingered in the form of the Russian Orthodox Church. Today, many of the churches built by Father Veniaminov and his missionaries still remain on the coasts of Alaska.

California and then west across the Pacific. La Perouse never returned to Alaska. In 1788, he and his ships were lost in a storm while searching for the Solomon Islands off of Australia.

As the nations of Europe sent out parties of explorers to investigate Alaska, the Russians moved east along the Aleutian Islands, collecting the pelts of sea otters, foxes, and seals. They paid little attention to the native Aleuts, until the Aleuts began to fight back as they saw their livelihood disappearing into the holds of Russian ships. The Alaska Natives lived on these animals, using nearly all the parts—hide, bones, teeth, blubber, flippers, sinews, and meat. The Russians traders wiped out entire animal populations for just their furs, leaving little or nothing left over for the Aleuts.

When the Aleuts protested the destruction of their way of life, the Russians, armed with guns, forced the Native people to work for them, hunting sea otters and other animals. With the Russian promyshlenniki—the fur hunters and trappers—came war, disease, and starvation that swept over the Aleut people. Within twenty-five years of their first contact with the hunters, only 20 percent of the Aleut population survived.

In the late 1750s, Stephen Glotov, a Russian fur trader, started trading peacefully with the Aleuts of Unimak and Unalaska Islands. Glotov's more organized and peaceful approach marked a change in Russia's dealings with Alaska. Russian trading companies began to replace the chaos of the individual hunters.

Gradually, the companies moved to subdue those who mistreated the Alaska Natives. In the 1790s, Aleksandr Baranov, head of the Shelikov-Golikov Company, discovered men from the Lebedev-Lastochikin Company were stealing furs, attacking women, and burning Aleut houses. Baranov sent eight of the men to Siberia to stand trial and brought in monks from the Russian Orthodox Church to minister to both the Russians and the Natives.

After the Empress Catherine the Great died in 1796, her son Paul granted the Shelikov-Golikov Company a trading monopoly in Alaska—something Catherine had refused to do. The other trading companies could either merge with them or disband. The new company became known as the Russian-American Company.

The Russian-American Company clashed with the Tlingit Indians when the company set

Retaliation means revenge.

Depleted means used up.

up their capital at Sitka, in the heart of Tlingit territory. The Tlingit attacked and killed most of 150 Russians and Aleuts on their first arrival in the Alexander Archipelago. In *retaliation*, the Russians attacked the Tlingit and drove them back from the area.

Over the years, Russia traded with both England and the United States for supplies and food. In 1854, however, the Crimean War broke out between Russia and Britain, ending their good relations. At this point, Alaska had become a drain on Russia's economy, taking more resources than it brought in. The fur trade had been *depleted* by constant overhunting, and Russia had not put any effort into harvesting Alaska's other resources. Russia's czar was beginning to look for an opportunity to get rid of his North American land. Once war began with Britain, however, Russia wanted to make sure the English did not get control of Alaska. The stage was set for the United States to purchase Alaska.

Tlingits canoing

Russian-American Company Contracts
Regulations Concerning Aleuts

- The Company will maintain the inhabitant of the Aleutian Islands in their present way of life.
- The inhabitants will be governed by their own native leaders and elders—supervised by Russian personnel appointed by the Company. Ultimate authority rests with the head administrative office.

Hunting:

- All male inhabitants of the Aleutian Islands from the ages of 18 to 50 are obligated to hunt sea animals for the Company.
- When hunting on their own (not with a company organized expedition) and using their own equipment and resources, all hunters must have permission of the authorities and may only sell their catch to the company.

Compensation:

- All hunters participating in a company sponsored expedition do not own the pelts of their catch, but instead receive a salary.
- When hunting on their own, all hunters will receive the following price for sea otter hides: Large hide: $5.00 Medium Hide: $2.00 Small Hide: $.50
- For work in the harbor or in the forest, Aleuts will receive $.50 per day.

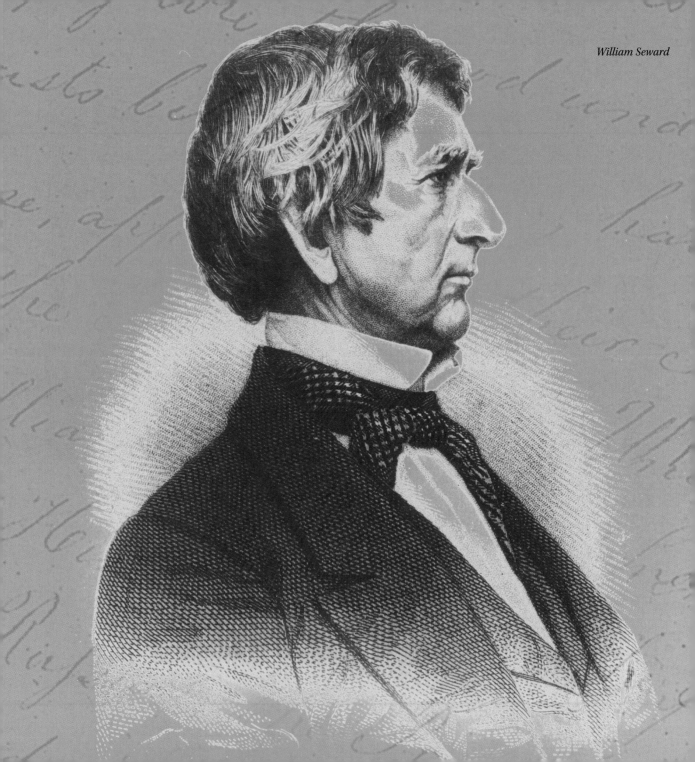

William Seward

Three
THE PURCHASE OF ALASKA

Late on the evening of March 30, 1867, Secretary of State William Seward unlocked the silent offices of the State Department and ushered the *delegation* of Russians inside. For months, Seward had been *negotiating* secretly with the Russian *minister* to the United States, Baron Edouard de Stoeckl. The year before, Stoeckl had approached Seward with a *proposal*, offering to sell Alaska—then known as Russian America—to the United States.

Even before he began talks with Stoeckl, Seward had dreamed of obtaining Alaska for the United States. The Civil War had just ended, however, and President Abraham Lincoln had been assassinated. The country was in upheaval, and politically, Seward's position was tricky. He was a member of the Republican Party, serving under President Andrew Johnson. Most of Congress disliked President Johnson, however; Seward had to proceed carefully if he was to acquire Alaska.

For this reason, Seward kept the purpose of his meetings with the Russians secret from Congress. During the early stages of negotiations, he had approached the *cabinet* and gotten authorization to offer seven million dollars for the land. Now, the details of the treaty had finally been agreed on. Russia was ready to transfer control of Alaska to the United States in exchange for $7,200,000. In his excitement, Seward did not want to wait even until morning

*A **delegation** is a group of people representing a larger organization or country.*

***Negotiating** means reaching a decision by a process of give-and-take.*

*A **minister** is a high government official or diplomatic representative.*

*A **proposal** is an offer.*

*A **cabinet** is a body of government advisers.*

Treaty of Cessation, 1867

44

to close the deal. He opened his office after hours, and he and Stoeckl signed the treaty. On June 27, President Johnson added his signature, approving the deal. Alaska had been purchased; now all that remained was getting Congress to approve the agreement.

The road to Alaska's purchase was overshadowed by the Reconstruction, the process of putting the country back together after the Civil War. War had splintered the United States, dividing North against South. Government leaders did not find it easy to **reintegrate** the Southern states. Northerners distrusted Southerners, and Southerners had their suspicions about Northerners as well. War had cost billions of dollars and Reconstruction added to that expense.

When Seward asked President Johnson's cabinet to authorize him to spend seven million dollars to purchase Alaska from the Russians, he was surprised when they agreed with very little argument. Seven million dollars was a lot of money, and most Americans, including the politicians, did not see any value in Alaska.

William Seward, however, had seen the value of Alaska for a long time. He believed the United States should expand its borders, gaining new land around the globe. Seward had served as the governor of New York and then as a United States Senator for New York. In 1860, he ran against Abraham Lincoln to gain the presidential nomination for the Republican Party. He lost to Lincoln, but when Lincoln became president, he appointed Seward as his secretary of state. As secretary of state, Seward was in charge of America's relationships with foreign countries. This position was

*To **integrate** means to join together into a unified whole, and reintegrate means to do it again, after a separation has occurred.*

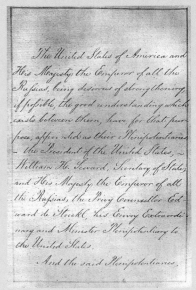

1st page of treaty ceding Alaska to the United States by Russia

ideal for him, as it gave him the opportunity to work toward gaining more territory for the United States.

Congress was taken aback when Seward presented them with the signed treaty. While some congressmen supported the idea, most were unhappy Seward had not brought the matter before them earlier. Congress debated the matter intensely for nearly a year, and the American public had their say as well. "What do we want with a bunch of ice and rocks?" newspapers asked, and most people agreed the money could be better spent elsewhere.

Although Congress took until July of 1868 to agree to pay Russia for the purchase of Alaska, they had very little choice in the matter. The treaty had been signed; on October 18, 1867, Russia had lowered its flag in Sitka, and the American flag had been raised in its place. Russian troops had left

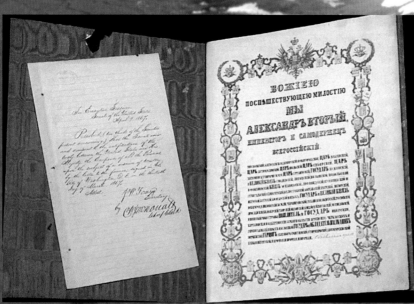

Russian treaty with senate clerk's ratification

Alaska. All that was left was for Congress to agree to give Russia its $7,200,000 in gold.

Antagonize means to annoy or to make angry.

The United States did not want to **antagonize** Russia by looking too hard for a way out of the treaty or by taking too long to pay for Alaska. The two countries had had a good relationship for many years, and Congress did not want to ruin the friendship by backing out of the Alaska purchase treaty. On July 27, 1868,

Alaska's Marmot Valley

47

The canceled U.S. check that was used to purchase Alaska

***Ceding** means transferring to another authority.*

Congress finally approved the purchase, releasing the treasury to pay Baron Stoeckl on behalf of Russia. They made sure, however, that they passed a law requiring future permission from Congress before large land purchases were made on behalf of the United States.

The treaty ***ceding*** Alaska to the United States gave Russians living in Alaska three years to return to Russia and keep their Russian citizenship. If they decided to stay in Alaska, however, they would be granted full rights as American citizens. The Alaska Natives did not receive any guarantee of citizenship.

The undersigned, Envoy Extraordinary and Minister Plenipotentiary
of His Majesty the Emperor of
the Russias, do hereby acknowledge
to have received at the Treasury Department in Washington _Seven_
Million Two hundred thousand dol-
lars ($7,200,000.) in coin, being the
full amount due from the United
States to Russia in consideration
of the cession, by the latter Power
to the former, of certain territory
described in the Treaty entered
into by the Emperor of all the Russias
and the President of the United States
on the 30th day of March 1867.—
Washington, August 1st 1868.

Stoeckl.

The receipt for Alaska's purchase

Joseph Juneau discovered gold in 1880, which spurred the development of a gold-mining town. The town of Juneau would one day become the state capital.

Log church, Juneau, 1888

For years after the territory of Alaska came under the control of the United States, the government did not quite know what to do with it. Less than a thousand white settlers lived in the entire area, and the federal government did not think this was enough to worry about setting up any kind of government. To make matters worse, these settlers did not impress government officials visiting Alaska. William Morris of the Treasury Department wrote:

> There are in this country as God-abandoned, God-forsaken, desperate, and rascally a set of wretches as can be found on earth. Their whole life is made up of fraud, deceit, lying, and thieving, and selling liquor to the Indians which they manufacture themselves.

The residents of Alaska were not politically unaware. They knew some form of government was needed. So, in 1881, they elected their own representatives and sent them to Washington, hoping that the federal government would take the hint. The representatives were mostly ignored in Washington, but their arrival did prompt lawmakers to take action—after another three years.

In 1884, the First Organic Act was passed.

A Forgotten State?

For thirty years after the United States purchased Alaska, the government seemed to forget it was there. It was sparsely populated, and since it wasn't causing any problems, they saw no real need to get involved in its day-to-day functioning. During those thirty years it was governed under military, naval, or military rule. Sometimes there was no ruling body at all. Then came the gold rush. More and more people traveled to Alaska to find their fortunes. Unfortunately, some fortune-seekers were interested in things less virtuous than working to discover gold. In 1900, in an attempt to strengthen the government, the capital was moved from Sitka to Juneau, and President McKinley divided the area into three judicial areas.

Alaska shortly after American purchase

51

The Organic Act created the District of Alaska, to be governed by officials the President would appoint. There were many problems with the act—for one thing, Alaskans themselves were given no voice in Washington—but it was a start, and a first, slow step toward statehood.

Sitka, 1805

52

Alaska Purchase Treaty (1867)

The inhabitants of the ceded territory, according to their choice, reserving their natural allegiance, may return to Russia within three years; but if they should prefer to remain in the ceded territory, they, with the exception of uncivilized native tribes, shall be admitted to the enjoyment of all the rights, advantages, and immunities of citizens of the United States, and shall be maintained and protected in the free enjoyment of their liberty, property, and religion. The uncivilized tribes will be subject to such laws and regulations as the United States may, from time to time, adopt in regard to aboriginal tribes of that country.

District Organic Treaty (1884)

Be it enacted by the Senate and House of Representatives of the United States of America in Congress assembled, That the territory ceded to the United States by Russia by the treaty of March thirtieth, eighteen hundred and sixty-seven and known as Alaska, shall constitute a civil and judicial district, the government of which shall be organized and administered as hereinafter provided. The temporary seat of government of said district is hereby established at Sitka.

John Muir

Four
ALASKA PROVES ITS WORTH

The morning of October 25, 1879, in Alaska's Alexander Archipelago was cold and rainy, with a bitter wind. John Muir, **_naturalist_**, scientist, and traveler, was setting out to see the ice mountains of which he had heard the Indians speak. At noon, they saw the first glacier. Muir looked up in awe at the mountain of ice towering above them. Later, in his book Travels in Alaska, he described the moment. "Its lofty blue cliffs, looming through the draggled skirts of the clouds, gave a tremendous impression of savage power," he wrote, "while the roar of the newborn icebergs thickened and emphasized the general roar of the storm."

The next day, Muir climbed alone to a peak overlooking the bay and saw below him five massive glaciers. The beauty he saw there and described later in his writings would attract millions of people, from Muir's time to today, to travel to Alaska simply for a glimpse of these towering walls of ice. Scientists came, too, to study the ice and how the glaciers moved.

*A **naturalist** is someone who is a field biologist; someone who studies biology in its natural state.*

Tourism was just one of the resources that the United States discovered unexpectedly in Alaska. Their new territory was not simply a frozen wasteland; money could be made there after all.

For over a century, the fur trade had been the main industry of white men in Alaska. The promyshlenniki had indiscriminately slaughtered millions of fur seals, sea otters, and other Alaskan animals. Finally, the first Russian governor in Alaska, Baron Ferdinand von Wrangell, in the early 1830s, realized that some of these animals could soon become extinct through overhunting. Von Wrangell set limits on the number of seals that could be killed in the Pribilof Islands, the main breeding grounds of the fur seals. This helped a little, but much damage had already been done.

When the United States took control of Alaska, the Alaska Commercial Company took over the fur industry from the Russian-American Company. The government regulated the company to some extent, limiting the number of seals hunters could kill to 100,000 a year, with no females or young pups to be included in the number. Whether hunters actually took the time to separate out the females and pups is doubtful.

The regulations imposed on the Alaska Commercial Company also required them to hire the local Aleuts and to provide them with free housing, education, and some free supplies. The Aleut hunters earned four cents per seal.

The United States found it difficult to control the number of seals killed when other countries also hunted in the area. To overcome this problem, America banned the other countries from hunting inside the three-mile limit marking United States territory. This did not work as well as the government had hoped, however. Instead of hunting the seals on land, ships sat just outside the three-mile limit and killed the seals swimming in the ocean. This *pelagic* sealing was an ongoing problem. It was not until 1911 that the Fur Seal Treaty between the United States, Great Britain, Russia, and Japan banned all pelagic sealing north of thirty degrees north latitude (south of California's southern border) across the whole North Pacific.

The Fur Seal Treaty also banned the hunting of sea otters, but by this time it was almost too late for these animals. By 1911, only around two thousand otters remained. In an attempt to protect them, large parts of the Aleutian Islands where they lived were named a wildlife refuge. Despite this effort, in 1925 a survey of the area found no otters at all and concluded that they had become extinct. In 1931, however, someone saw a mother sea otter with her pup. Since that time, the sea otter population has begun to increase.

Seals cannot be hunted when they are swimming at sea in the North Pacific

Earlier Russian, British, Spanish, and French expeditions had mapped nearly all of Alaska's coastlines. John Muir, visiting Glacier Bay, had filled in the last uncharted piece of the southern coast. Huge portions of the interior, however, still remained blank on maps.

Pelagic *means occurring on the open sea.*

57

In the early 1880s, the U.S. Army sent out several groups to explore and map the rivers around the upper Yukon River. These first expeditions expanded existing maps and increased the public's awareness of Alaska's geography by publishing reports of their travels in popular magazines.

In March of 1885, another expedition embarked. Lieutenant Henry Allen, together with Sergeant Cady Robertson and Private Frederick Fickett, set out to explore and map the region between the Yukon River and the Gulf of Alaska. This was a huge area, but they succeeded. Fifteen hundred miles later, they had traveled up the Copper River, along the Tanana River to the Yukon, and then north again up the Koyukuk River. Few people have heard of these men, but they have been credited with adding more to the knowledge about Alaska than any other team of explorers.

Many Americans first realized the purchase of Alaska might not have been so crazy after all in 1896, when gold was discovered along the Klondike River in Canada. Suddenly, people were flocking to Alaska to travel to the Klondike. Then, prospectors started looking for gold in Alaska as well. If there was gold in the Klondike, there could be could be gold other places too. Hopeful gold-seekers swarmed across Alaska, looking in rivers, on beaches, up and down the hills and mountains. The population of Alaska suddenly exploded; tens of thousands of new people came and stayed, building towns and roads. The crowded camps of frenzied prospectors also brought crime and disorder. President William McKinley began to realize that with more people, Alaska was going to need a stronger government and more laws.

Another resource Americans discovered in Alaska was salmon. For thousands of years, the eastern and inland Alaska Natives had been living off the salmon in their rivers. In 1878, the first cannery opened on Prince of Wales Island

Goldminers holding gold

58

Otters were also hunted for their fur

Strategic means characteristic of the science and art of military command to meet the enemy in combat under advantageous conditions.

Pivotal means vitally important.

Casualties are injuries and deaths in war.

Industrialized means made into an area that supports, and is supported by, industry.

Cannery, Hoohnah 1917

in the southeasternmost part of Alaska. Hundreds of thousands of cases of salmon were processed here and at other canneries. For years the canneries, and the officials who were eventually sent to regulate them, ignored warnings that overfishing would destroy the salmon population. By 1911, the salmon runs had dwindled to a fraction of the size they had once been.

In 1922, President Warren G. Harding finally established fishing reserves to protect the salmon. People would need to get permits if they wanted to catch salmon in these areas. Problems with the system became apparent immediately, however. Most of the available permits went to the canneries, while Native people who relied on the salmon to live became the ones banned from fishing. The government adjusted the permit system slightly, but it was not until Alaska became a state and could make its own laws that the Native people were able to resolve the salmon issues to their own satisfaction.

One of Alaska's benefits Americans could not have foreseen was its **strategic** military position. Toward the beginning of World War II, the American government started to become aware of the need to build up Alaska's defenses. President Franklin Roosevelt realized that Alaska could all too easily become a steppingstone to an enemy presence on North America. Much of Alaska was remote; Japanese forces could arrive and set up bases before Americans even realized they were there. A National Geographic article reported that Japanese and German groups had been walking around Alaska.

In response to the threat, the United States and Canada built a series of runways across Canada and throughout Alaska. Several army regiments would spend nearly the entire war in Alaska, building roads to connect these landing areas. Pipelines would be built to transport oil from Canada to Alaska, so that Alaska would be less reliant on ships for oil.

In 1942, the Americans bombed Tokyo, sending the bombers from a carrier at sea. The Japanese, however, thought the planes must have been sent from a base in Alaska. They set out to destroy the base and establish their own presence on American soil. The mission was also supposed to serve as a diversion from Japan's main attack on Midway Island. In fact, instead of diverting the American focus from the attack on Midway, Japan's campaign in Alaska actually distracted Japanese attention and troops away from the central Pacific, and the Americans were able to win the *pivotal* Battle of Midway.

Japanese forces managed to occupy the Aleutian Islands on Attu and Kiska, on the western tip of the island chain, just east of the International Date Line. The islands are so remote the United States did not immediately notice Japan's presence, as had been feared. When

Cold War battleships

they did realize the Japanese had occupied the islands, months passed before Americans were able to begin to retake them. Storms slowed the process, as well as the fact that American forces needed first to build airfields on nearby islands from which to send out bombers to attack the Japanese. After difficult battle and many *casualties*, the United States was finally able to retake the islands in the summer of 1943. Since bases and airfields now existed in the western Aleutians, American forces were able to use them to attack Japan's northernmost territory, the Kurile Islands, just south of Kamchatka.

During World War II, Alaska found itself suddenly *industrialized*. Roads and airfields now

The Cold War *was a conflict of ideas and beliefs between the United States and the U.S.S.R. carried out by methods just short of sustained military action.*

Franklin Roosevelt

connected remote areas, and military bases along the coasts housed thousands of people. Over the next decades, the population of Alaska would nearly double.

Alaska's location became even more important from a military point of view during the ***Cold War***. The United States and the U.S.S.R. had been allies during World War II, but their relationship changed, and tensions between the two countries remained high for many years. The North American Air Defense Command (NORAD) built radar stations across Alaska to detect any incoming missiles from Soviet Russia.

The strained relations between the United States and the U.S.S.R. during the Cold War actually helped Alaska's economy. With money pouring into the area for defense, Alaska was able to grow and develop to a greater extent than ever before.

One of the changes brought to Alaska after World War II was the growth of the logging industry. When the United States first purchased Alaska from Russia, the American government restricted logging in the new territory, so as not to interfere with the industry in

An Aleut takes refuge in a sod house

Aleuts During World War II

In 1942, Japanese Americans were rounded up and put in internment camps, for fear they would suddenly turn on the United States. At the same time, but not so well known, the U.S. government ordered that anyone in Alaska with one-eighth Aleut blood or more be evacuated. As a result, 881 Aleut people were removed from their homes in the western Aleutian and Pribilof Islands, presumably for their own safety but for military reasons as well, and relocated to southeast Alaska. Unlike the Japanese Americans, however, the Aleuts could leave, but most had no place to go and remained in these "duration villages" until 1945. Many Aleut villages were then burned to make way for military operations.

A number of young Aleut men did enlist in the military, however. Several regiments of Alaska Natives served during the war, including the Alaska Scouts, a special commando unit led by intelligence officer Lawrence Castner and nicknamed "Castner's Cutthroats."

Clear-cut land

*To **clear-cut** means to re-move all trees.*

other parts of America. This restriction was partially lifted at the beginning of the twentieth century, but it was not until the late 1940s that logging took off as an industry in Alaska.

Logging helped the economy, but there were problems with it as well. Loggers clear-cut huge tracts of forest and the Tlingit and Haida Indians objected. This was their land, they claimed. In the early 1970s, the Native tribes received a section of the Tongass Forest and then proceeded to ***clear-cut*** it themselves for the profit.

John Muir Sees Glacier Bay for the First Time

(from *Travels in Alaska*, Chapter 10: The Discovery of Glacier Bay)

The next day being Sunday, the minister wished to stay in camp; and so, on account of the weather, did the Indians. I therefore set out on an excursion, and spent the day alone on the mountain-slopes above the camp, and northward, to see what I might learn. Pushing on through rain and mud and sludgy snow, crossing many brown, boulder-choked torrents, wading, jumping, and wallowing in snow up to my shoulders was mountaineering of the most trying kind. After crouching cramped and benumbed in the canoe, poulticed in wet or damp clothing night and day, my limbs had been asleep. This day they were awakened and in the hour of trial proved that they had not lost the cunning learned on many a mountain peak of the High Sierra. I reached a height of fifteen hundred feet, on the ridge that bounds the second of the great glaciers. All the landscape was smothered in clouds and I began to fear that as far as wide views were concerned I had climbed in vain. But at length the clouds lifted a little, and beneath their gray fringes I saw the berg-filled expanse of the bay, and the feet of the mountains that stand about it, and the imposing fronts of five huge glaciers, the nearest being immediately beneath me. This was my first general view of Glacier Bay, a solitude of ice and snow and newborn rocks, dim, dreary, mysterious. I held the ground I had so dearly won for an hour or two, sheltering myself from the blast as best I could, while with benumbed fingers I sketched what I could see of the landscape, and wrote a few lines in my notebook. Then, breasting the snow again, crossing the shifting avalanche slopes and torrents, I reached camp about dark, wet and weary and glad.

Alaska has many natural resources—seals, salmon, and timber are some of these. These resources seemed limitless to explorers and settlers, but they were not, of course. Unfortunately, the pattern has too often been that a certain resource was overhunted or overused until it was nearly destroyed. Sea otters nearly became extinct, and other species did become extinct, such as the spectacled cormorant and the sea cow discovered by Georg Steller. Salmon runs shrank as the canneries harvested increasing numbers of salmon, until the federal government stepped in to control overfishing.

Today, conservation groups keep a close watch on Alaska, fighting against the clear-cutting of forests and working to keep Alaskan wildlife from extinction. Alaska does have many natural resources—but all too easily they can be lost by overuse.

Salmon

Dwight D. Eisenhower

Five
THE FORTY-NINTH STATE

The citizens of Alaska were tired of not having any say in the laws that governed them.

Corporations controlled most of Alaska's resources and, therefore, its economy. Alaska could not collect taxes of its own to spend on building hospitals or schools. When Alaskans wanted something done, they had to *petition* the federal government in Washington, D.C. Washington politicians had a lot of other issues to handle, and Alaska was not usually at the head of the list. Furthermore, lawmakers often cared about different things than Alaskans. The laws they made did not always reflect the values and concerns of the Alaskan people.

On March 30, 1916, a bill to make Alaska a state was introduced in the House of Representatives. The bill was put aside and nearly forgotten by politicians, however, as World War I, the *Great Depression*, and then World War II gripped the attention of the country.

*To **petition** means to formally ask for something, usually in writing.*

*The **Great Depression** was a period from the late 1920s to the 1930s characterized by extreme unemployment and low economic activity.*

69

Alaska's state flower, the forget-me-not

When World War II ended, the issue of statehood for Alaska came up again. The secretary of Alaska, Edward Lewis "Bob" Bartlett, and the governor of Alaska, Ernest Gruening, fought to convince Congress that Alaska should be made a state. In 1949, the Alaska Statehood Committee formed. Then, in the early 1950s, Operation Statehood began. Before the question of Alaska's statehood was to be discussed, legislators received bouquets of artificial forget-me-nots, Alaska's official flower. Alaskans also sent out Christmas cards to their friends in the rest of the United States that read:

Make our future bright
Ask your Senator for statehood
And start the New Year right!

Alaska's state seal

The American public generally supported statehood for Alaska, but politicians still had concerns. They worried that Alaskan politicians would be too far removed from the issues that faced most of the lower forty-eight states. Senators from heavily populated states did not like the idea that Alaska would have the same amount of power in the Senate as they did, even though Alaska's population was so small.

In President Dwight Eisenhower's 1954 State of the Union address, he asked for immediate statehood for Hawaii, but made no mention of Alaska. Hawaii tended to follow the ideas of the Republican Party, while Alaska was more Democratic. Eisenhower's Republican administration was more interested in admitting a state to the Union that would support their political party's actions.

To satisfy Alaskans, the Senate proposed a

*A **constitutional convention** is a formal meeting organized to develop a written set of laws to govern a body.*

Alaska's rugged mountains

bill that would first admit Hawaii as a state, and then Alaska. Alaskans were not satisfied. They were tired of waiting and wanted statehood right away.

In 1955, Alaskans elected their own delegates to a ***constitutional convention.*** Over seventy-five days, fifty-five delegates drafted a state constitution. The opening of the constitution read:

> We the people of Alaska, grateful to God and to those who founded our nation and pioneered this great land, in order to secure and transmit to succeeding generations our heritage of political, civil, and religious liberty within the Union of States, do ordain and establish this constitution for the State of Alaska.

In 1956, Alaskans voted to accept the new constitution. The same spring, they elected Ernest Gruening and William Egan as their United States Senators and Ralph J. Rivers to the House of Representatives. The men traveled to Washington, where the press and the public welcomed them with excitement. Congress, however, did not recognize their positions, and they were not allowed to take up their elected roles.

In 1958, President Eisenhower finally recommended Alaska for statehood. Congress recognized Alaska's constitution and introduced bills to make Alaska a state. On May 26, 1958, the House of Representatives passed the Alaska Statehood Bill. On June 30, the bill passed in the Senate, with a vote of 64 to 20.

Finally, on January 3, 1959, President Eisenhower signed the declaration that made Alaska the forty-ninth state of the United States.

Alaska's state flag

73

WHAT THE LAND MEANS TO AMERICANS

The American and Alaskan flags

In the time leading up to statehood, many groups of Alaska Natives had made requests for land of their own. The Alaska Statehood Act mentioned these land claims, but only briefly. The act stated that Alaska did not own the land claimed by the Native peoples, instead, it was holding it in trust for them. How much land belonged to the Alaska Natives, however, and where exactly this land was located, were not mentioned in the Statehood Act. That issue would be dealt with at another time.

In 1959, Alaska adopted its state flag, the yellow stars of the Big Dipper and the North Star on a deep, blue background. In 1927, the Alaska Department of the American Legion had sponsored a contest for students in grades seven through twelve to design a flag for Alaska. The winner was Benny Benson, a thirteen-year-old Aleut living in an orphanage in Seward. In his contest entry, Benny sent a drawing of the flag and wrote, "The blue field is for the sky and the Forget-Me-Not, the state flower. The North Star is for the future of the state of Alaska, the most northerly of the Union. The dipper is for the Great Bear—symbolizing strength." Benny received a thousand dollars for winning the contest, which the American Legion put toward his education.

Alaska's state song was written in 1955 by Marie Drake. Called "Alaska's Flag," the words of the song echo Benny Benson's description of the flag's meaning.

> *Eight stars of gold on a field of blue—*
> *Alaska's flag. May it mean to you*
> *The blue of the sea, the evening sky,*
> *The mountain lakes, and the flow'rs nearby;*
> *The gold of the early sourdough's dreams,*
> *The precious gold of the hills and streams;*
> *The brilliant stars in the northern sky,*
> *The "Bear"—the "Dipper"—and, shining high,*
> *The great North Star with its steady light,*
> *Over land and sea a beacon bright.*
> *Alaska's flag—to Alaskans dear,*
> *The simple flag of a last frontier.*

Alaska is so large that it can hold the twenty-one smallest states. When a scale map of Alaska is placed over one for the lower forty-eight states, Alaska stretches from coast to coast.

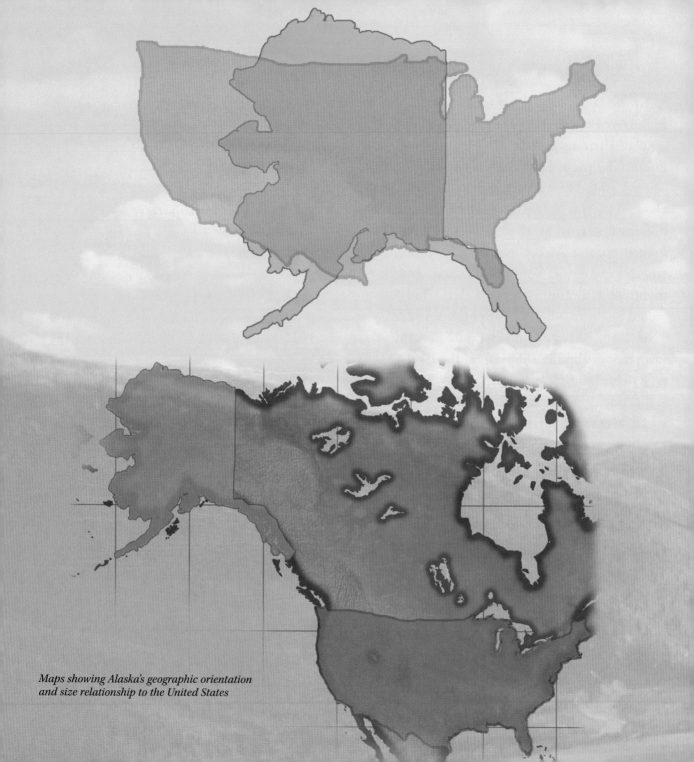

*Maps showing Alaska's geographic orientation
and size relationship to the United States*

Six

ALASKA TODAY

The officers of the *Exxon Valdez* oil tanker got out of the cab and walked toward their ship. They had spent most of the day of March 23, 1989, in the town of Valdez, Alaska, but now they were about to leave with a full load of oil bound for Long Beach, California. Earlier in the day, the captain, Joseph Hazelwood, had taken care of some ship's business and then gone to a bar with some of the other officers. He had a few drinks, but neither the cab driver nor the security guard that let the officers into the shipyard thought the captain seemed drunk.

Getting out of Valdez Narrows could be tricky, so the harbor pilot, Ed Murphy, steered the tanker out of the Narrows. At a little before 11:30 P.M., the *Exxon Valdez* had cleared the harbor, and Murphy left to take another boat back to port.

Shipping regulations stated that incoming and outgoing oil tankers must keep within a certain area. This made sure that they stayed in deep waters and out of each other's way. On this night, however, small icebergs floated in the shipping lane ahead of the *Exxon Valdez*. To avoid them, Captain Hazelwood ordered a change of course, taking the tanker out of its lane and all the way across the lane for incoming ships. It had been a long day, and Captain Hazelwood left the bridge, leaving Third Mate Gregory Cousins in charge.

Cousins' shift was supposed to end at midnight when the second mate would take over. Cousins knew the second mate had worked hard that day, though, helping to load the ship.

Negligent *means done without proper care or caution.*

Environmentalists *are people who care for and act on behalf of the environment.*

The **permafrost** *is a permanently frozen layer at variable depths below the surface in frigid regions of a planet.*

Cleaning up after an oil spill

Instead of calling him at midnight, Cousins decided to let him sleep.

At this point, Cousins was the only officer on the bridge, although company policy stated there should always be at least two. Cousins was tired as well; later reports suggested he might actually have been working for eighteen hours straight by this time.

Suddenly, the lookout noticed the Bligh Reef light was on the wrong side of the ship. That meant the *Exxon Valdez* was headed straight for the rocks of the reef. She called up to the bridge, but Cousins was already making the course corrections.

Unfortunately, he did not change the ship's direction soon enough. At 12:04 A.M. on March 24, 1989, the *Exxon Valdez* ran aground on Bligh Reef, spilling 11 million gallons of oil into the waters of Prince William Sound. The result was one of the worst spills in American history, costing over two billion dollars in cleanup and killing hundreds of thousands of birds and sea animals. From an environmental viewpoint, the *Exxon Valdez* oil spill was the worst the world has seen.

After its investigation of the accident, the National Transportation Safety Board laid the blame on a number of factors, including the captain's possible impairment from alcohol and the third mate's possible fatigue and overwork. Captain Hazelwood was later tried, and a jury found him not guilty of operating a vessel while under the influence of alcohol. He was, however, fined $50,000 and sentenced to one thousand hours of community service for **negligent** discharge of oil.

The discovery of oil in Prudhoe Bay in 1968 led to greatly in-

The Alaska pipeline

creased Alaskan wealth—and serious environmental concerns. The Prudhoe Bay oil field was the richest ever discovered in the United States. However, its location on the frozen north coast of Alaska meant major steps would have to be taken to transport the oil south. Oil companies proposed a variety of ideas, including moving the oil by railroad, ships, submarines, or giant air tankers. The favorite idea was to construct a giant pipeline running across the interior of Alaska to Valdez on the south coast.

Environmentalists raised many concerns about the effects both drilling and transporting the oil could have on the environment. Usually, pipelines were buried, but the hot oil in the pipe would keep the ***permafrost*** around it from freezing if it were buried.

Finally, in 1973, Congress voted to allow the construction of an overland pipeline. The pipe would not be buried in the ground, but would be elevated slightly over it. In March 1975, construction began. Over 70,000 people contributed to its construction before the pipeline was completed in April 1977.

79

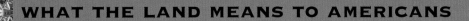
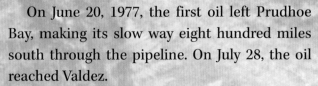

On June 20, 1977, the first oil left Prudhoe Bay, making its slow way eight hundred miles south through the pipeline. On July 28, the oil reached Valdez.

Much of the reason it had taken nearly ten years from the time oil was discovered at Prudhoe to the completion of the pipeline was that the question of Native land claims had not been resolved. Before the oil companies could build their pipeline across Alaska, they needed to know exactly which land belonged to the Native peoples. In a way, this meant the discovery of oil was a good thing for the Alaska Natives. The oil companies and the U.S. government were suddenly eager to resolve the problem.

In 1971, the Alaska Native Claims Settlement Act (ANCSA) gave the Alaska Natives approxi-

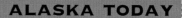

mately one-ninth of the state's land—43.7 million acres—and nearly a billion dollars in compensation. ANCSA land was divided into twelve regions, each governed by a Native corporation. The Alaska Natives now could make decisions about what happened on their own land.

Environmentalists were concerned that too much of Alaska was in danger of becoming developed. As a result, ANCSA included an agreement that the Department of the Interior would take 80 million acres of federal lands and study them to decide which parts should become national parks, national forests, and wildlife refuges.

A time limit had been set for the creation of these lands. If, after the time expired, no lands had been chosen, the entire area would be reopened for development. Time was running out

1980, Congress drafted its own bill, adding even more land. On December 2, 1980, President Carter signed the Alaska National Interest Lands Conservation Act (ANILCA). ANILCA added over 53 million acres to the National Wildlife Refuge System, over 56 million acres to the National Wilderness Preservation system, and over 43 million acres to the National Park System. These additions doubled the size of the country's National Park and Refuge System and tripled the size of the designated wilderness areas.

In 1953, an article by the Sierra Club called "Northeast Arctic: The Last Great Wilderness" led to the creation of the Arctic National Wildlife Range in 1960. The area was considered the last truly untouched wilderness area in the world. In 1980, ANILCA brought the size of the area up to 19 million acres and changed the name to the Arctic National Wildlife Refuge. ANILCA also left open the possibility for oil and gas development of certain sections of the Arctic National Wildlife Refuge.

Today, whether or not to drill for oil on the Wildlife Refuge is an ongoing debate. A 1998 United States Geological Survey determined that even more oil than had previously been

Native statue

and still nothing had been decided. To keep the area closed from developers, President Jimmy Carter chose 56 million acres and made them national monuments. Finally, in the summer of

thought was present in the area. Conservationists point to the environmental effects drilling would have on the area; supporters of the idea claim that damage to the environment would be extremely limited.

Those on both sides of the issue use emotional arguments to sway the public. A video on the Web site for the Defenders of Wildlife shows polar bears rolling and playing on Alaska's Coastal Plain, the area of proposed drilling. On the other hand, the secretary of the interior, testifying before the House Committee on Resources in 2003, referred to the area as "flat, white nothingness" and described it as having "56 days of total darkness during the year, and almost nine months of harsh winter," as well as wind chills of minus 75 degrees Fahrenheit (59 degrees Celsius).

The continuing question in Alaska is this: "To whom does the land belong?" Author Walter Borneman writes that "In the final analysis, the land belongs to all of us, and yet to none of us." Although this may be the truth, it is difficult to know how it translates into specific answers for issues such as drilling on the Arctic National Wildlife Refuge. In the end, economic factors must be balanced with environmental ones.

Even after the present drilling issue has been resolved, other debates will certainly arise to make us consider our relationship with the land. The question of to whom the land belongs will always be with us, forcing us to examine our place in the world.

Nugget Pond

Alaska National Interest Land Conservation Act (1980)

Lands added to the National Parks and Preserves (in acres):

Aniakchak National Monument	138,000
Aniakchak National Preserve	376,000
Bering Land Bridge National Preserve	2,457,000
Cape Krustenstern National Monument	560,000
Gates of the Arctic National Park	7,052,000
Gates of the Arctic National Preserve	900,000
Kenai Fjords National Park	570,000
Kobuk Valley National Park	1,710,000
Lake Clark National Park	2,439,000
Lake Clark National Preserve	1,214,000
Noatak National Preserve	6,460,000
Wrangell-Saint Elias National Park	8,147,000
Wrangell-Saint Elias National Preserve	4,171,000
Yukon-Charley Rivers National Preserve	1,713,000
Glacier Bay National Park additions	523,000
Glacier Bay National Preserve	57,000
Katmai National Park additions	1,037,000
Katmai National Preserve	308,000
Denali (Mount McKinley) National Park additions	2,426,000
Denali National Preserve	1,330,000

Alaska National Interest Land Conservation Act (1980)

The 19.6 million-acre Arctic National Wildlife Refuge (ANWR), located in the northeast corner of Alaska, is tundra with spots of marshes and lagoon. Rivers flow between the mountains of the Brooks Range and the Beaufort Sea. It is home to 160 bird species, the denning area for polar bears, and the primary calving area for the Porcupine caribou herd. Grizzly bears, wolves, arctic foxes, and whales also find homes here.

Why would such a beautiful area be the subject of controversy? Oil. Some believe that these animals share their home with enough oil so that, those in favor of a bill in the House claim, the United States could reduce its importation of foreign oil by 20 percent by the year 2025.

The current bill in the House of Representatives would open two thousand acres of the ANWR to drilling. Proponents of the bill claim that drilling, in addition to reducing the U.S. dependency on foreign oil, would create 800,000 to 1.3 million new jobs and lower the prices of gasoline. Those against drilling say that the bill's proponents exaggerate the number of jobs that would be created and that the answers to the continuing oil problems in the United States are to be found in conservation, development of alternative fuels, and improved efficiency in products such as air conditioners and motor vehicles. They point out that, despite high gasoline prices, people are still purchasing SUVs. According to the bill's opponents, the United States sits on 3 percent of the world's oil reserves yet uses 25 percent.

A bill to allow drilling in the ANWR passed the House and the Senate in 1995. It was vetoed by President Bill Clinton. The House passed a bill allowing drilling in 2001 and 2003, but it failed in the Senate both times.

1725 Czar Peter the Great commissions Vitus Bering, to discover whether or not Russia is connected to North America.

28,000 13,000 B.C. Native Peoples migrate across the Bering Land Bridge to North America during the last ice age.

1741 Bering makes his second voyage to the islands off the coast of Alaska.

1728 Bering makes his first voyage through the Bering Strait.

1648 Semenn Ivanovitch Dezhnev explores the area between Siberia and Russia.pendence.

March 30, 1867 Secretary of State William Seward, acting on behalf of the United States government, purchases the territory of Alaska from the Russians.

October 25, 1879 Naturalist John Muir discovers Glacier Bay.

March 30, 1916 First Alaska Statehood Bill introduced in the House of Representatives.

July 27, 1868 Congress finally approves the purchase of Alaska.

1896 Gold is discovered in the Yukon River in Canada.

1796 Shelikov-Golikov Company granted a trading monopoly in Alaska. The other trading companies merge with it. The company changes its name to the Russian-American Company.

1955 Alaska drafts its own constitution.

Summer 1943 American troops retake Attu and Kiska.

1922 President Harding establishes fishing reserves.

January 3, 1959 Alaska joins the United States as the 49th state.

1956 Alaska elects United States Senators and a Representative and sends the men to Washington.

1942 During the Second World War, Japanese forces take Attu and Kiska Islands, at the end of the Aleutian chain.

1949 Alaska Statehood Committee forms to fight to make Alaska a state.

1971 Alaska Natives Claims Settlement Act gives the Alaska Natives 43.7 million acres of land.

2001, 2003 The House of Representatives passes a bill allowing oil drilling in the Arctic National Wildlife Refuge, but it failed in the Senate both times.

December 2, 1980 The Alaska National Interest Lands Conservation Act adds millions of acres to the National Parks and Wildlife Refuges.

1977 The Trans-Alaska Pipeline system begins carrying oil 800 miles south from Prudhoe Bay to Valdez.

March 24, 1989 The *Exxon Valdez* runs aground, spilling 11 million gallons of oil into Prince William Sound. A massive cleanup effort follows.

1968 Oil is discovered in Prudhoe Bay.

FURTHER READING

Chevigny, Hector. *Russian America: The Great Alaskan Venture, 1741–1867.* New York: Viking Press, 1965.

Cohen, Daniel. *The Alaska Purchase.* Brookfield, Conn.: Millbrook Press, 1996.

Dunnahoo, Terry. *Alaska.* New York: Franklin Watts, 1987.

Ford, Corey. *Where the Sea Breaks Its Back.* Boston: Little, Brown and Company, 1966.

Horn, Gabriel. *Steller's Sea Cow.* New York: Crestwood House, 1989.

Hoyt-Goldsmith, Diane. *Arctic Hunter.* New York: Holiday House, 1992.

Hunt, William R. *Alaska: A Bicentennial History.* New York: W. W. Norton & Company, 1976.

Kendall, Russ. *Eskimo Boy: Life in an Inupiaq Eskimo Village.* New York: Scholastic, 1992.

Mathews, Richard. *The Yukon.* New York: Holt, Rinehart and Winston, 1968.

McNeer, May. *The Alaska Gold Rush.* New York: Random House, 1960.

Melbo, Irving Robert. *Our Country's National Parks, Volume Two: 50 States Edition.* Indianapolis, Ind.: Bobbs-Merrill Company, 1961.

Muir, John. *All the World Over: Notes from Alaska.* San Francisco: Sierra Club Books, 1996.

Patent, Dorothy Hinshaw. *Places of Refuge: Our National Wildlife Refuge System.* New York: Clarion Books, 1992.

Schurke, Paul. *Bering Bridge: The Soviet-American Expedition from Siberia to Alaska.* Duluth, Minn.: Pfeifer-Hamilton, 1989.

Somervill, Barbara. *Alaska.* New York: Children's Press, 2002.

Strohmeyer, John. *Extreme Conditions: Big Oil and the Transformation of Alaska.* New York: Simon & Schuster, 1993.

Thompson, Kathleen. *Alaska.* Milwaukee, Wis.: Raintree, 1988.

Webb, Nancy McIvor. *Aguk of Alaska.* Englewood Cliffs, N.J.: Prentice-Hall, 1963.

Whitcraft, Melissa. *Seward's Folly.* New York: Children's Press, 2002.

FOR MORE INFORMATION

Alaska Information
www.everythingalaska.com

Alaska Natives
www.alaskanative.net

Alaska Explorers
www.explorenorth.com/library/history/
geodic-ak-1902

Alaska Statehood
www.alaska.edu/creatingalaska

Alaska National Wildlife Refuge
www.arctic.fws.gov

Publisher's note:
The Web sites listed on this page were active at the time of publication. The publisher is not responsible for Web sites that have changed their addresses or discontinued operation since the date of publication. The publisher will review and update the Web sites upon each reprint.

INDEX

BIOGRAPHIES

AUTHOR

Sheila Nelson has always been fascinated with history and the lives of historical figures. When she was twelve years old, she memorized Longfellow's poem, "Paul Revere's Ride," after she realized the event had taken place on her birthday. Later, she was able to study history more formally and enjoyed learning more about the events and people that have shaped our world. Sheila recently completed a master's degree and now lives in Rochester, New York, with her husband and their baby daughter. She has written several other titles in this series.

SERIES CONSULTANT

Dr. Jack N. Rakove is a professor of history and American studies at Stanford University, where he is director of American studies. The winner of the 1997 Pulitzer Prize in history, Dr. Rakove is the author of *The Unfinished Election of 2000, Constitutional Culture and Democratic Rule,* and *James Madison and the Creation of the American Republic.* He is also the president of the Society for the History of the Early American Republic.

PICTURE CREDITS

Alaska Historical Collection: pp. 12–13, 15, 30, 32, 33, 42, 44, 50, 52–53, 58, 60, 69
Alaska State Library: pp. 21, 23, 62–63
Artville: p. 11
Corel: cover, pp. 8–9, 14, 16–17, 18–19, 24–25, 27, 28–29, 38, 46–47, 54–55, 66–67, 72, 74, 74–75, 76–77, 80–81, 82, 83, 84–85, 86–87, 88–89, 98
Dalhousie University: p. 20
Dover: p. 10
Map Resources: p. 76
National Archives: pp. 51, 62
PhotoDisc: pp. 64, 78, 79
Photos.Com: pp. 31, 32, 33, 57, 59